T0197594

Your Greatest Greatness

Tapping Into Your True Potential

By: Barry E. Ward II

Illustrations by Joshua Allen

AuthorHouse™
1663 Liberty Drive
Bloomington, IN 47403
www.authorhouse.com
Phone: 1 (833) 262-8899

Because of the dynamic nature of the Internet, any web addresses or links contained in this book may have changed since publication and may no longer be valid. The views expressed in this work are solely those of the author and do not necessarily reflect the views of the publisher, and the publisher hereby disclaims any responsibility for them.

Any people depicted in stock imagery provided by Getty Images are models, and such images are being used for illustrative purposes only.
Certain stock imagery © Getty Images.

This book is printed on acid-free paper.

ISBN: 978-1-4490-7839-3 (sc)

Library of Congress Control Number: 2010900775

Print information available on the last page.

Published by AuthorHouse 10/19/2020

authorHOUSE

This book is dedicated to my beautiful and talented mother, Elaine A. Ward.

Gratitude is funny in a sense that when a time presents itself to truly show it, no words seem good enough. No emotions seem real enough. No kind of sweet gesture can really illustrate its true essence. Mom, from the depths of my soul, I say thank you and I love you. Because of you and your love for me, I found my **"Greatest Greatness."**

We have been waiting for U.

U are special.

U have something that we need.

Are
U
Ready?

Are U Sure?

U are special.

Maybe
U
        didn't

                know.

What
is
your
biggest
Dream?

Don't
Say
IT
Aloud!

Stop
and

think

about

<u>IT</u>.

Don't share that dream with just anyone.

Do U dream and

then wish for your dreams to come true?

Have U ever wished for something and after U wished for it, U made another wish for your first wish to come true?

Little faith makes a little U.

Did U know?

U are greater than

U know, but first

U have to let <u>IT</u> go.

Let

IT

Go!

U don't know what that IT is?

I think U do.

It's the same __IT__ that has been holding U back this entire time.

Let

__IT__

Go!

The world could be yours.

Is **IT** too big?

Are u too small?

There
is
something
great
inside
of
U.

Why
haven't
U
looked for IT?

Look Left!

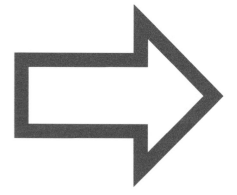

Look Right!

Look Up!

Look Down!

U don't see IT?

Everyone Else Does.

Look at yourself and
Say IT!

Say

I

Am

Great!

U want to say it, don't hold back.

-COME ON-

SAY

I

AM

GREAT!

SAY
IT
AGAIN!

LOUDER!

Do U feel that tingle inside?

That is your "Greatest Greatness" and it's ready to burst out.

SAY

IT

One more time!

Say

I

AM

GREAT!

We have been waiting for <u>IT</u> and U have had <u>IT</u> this entire time!

Can we have <u>IT</u>?

U found IT!

I knew

U

were special!

Now go and share your
"Greatest Greatness"
with the rest of
the world.

THE
END

Be careful when sharing your "Big Dreams" with "little people."

When I mention "little people," I am referring to individuals who discourage U. Who laugh at your ideas. Who try to pull U down. They do this to try to gain an understanding of your "Greatness." Your ideas and goals are beyond their small vision.

Make it a habit to surround yourself with people that speak life into your "Greatness." U must spend every minute of everyday enhancing and tweaking the things that make U better than U were yesterday.

In order for U to truly find your "Greatest Greatness," U must share your dreams with people who recognize that U are bursting with potential. The space that U occupy is filled with an untapped talent that only you possess. U are greater than U know, but first U have to let your Greatness Grow, then "LET IT Go!"

"One of the hardest things to do is to forgive yourself for not doing something U wish U had done." - Barry E. Ward II

About the Author

Barry E. Ward II was born in Houston, Texas into a loving and encouraging family. He has been named one of Houston's "Top Educators," and he takes pride in his ability to reach the children that have been labeled as, "unteachable." Barry currently serves as an Administrator on the Northwest Side of Houston. He is deeply rooted in his community and devotes his life to helping children reach their full potential. He enjoys sports, reading, writing, and spending time with his beautiful family. Barry is currently working on his PhD in Education at a prestigious university in Texas.

Book Preview

There are billions of people on this planet. However, there is no one else that is just like you. **YOU ARE SPECIAL.** This book was written to help readers realize the space that they occupy is bursting with potential. <u>Your Greatest Greatness</u> motivates readers to spend every minute improving the things today that will make them better than they were yesterday. Filled with deep and meaningful illustrations, this book inspires readers to realize that we all have everything we need to achieve everything we want, **Right Now**. That thing is your "Greatest Greatness." NOW LET "<u>IT</u>" GO!

Printed in the United States
By Bookmasters